A Story of HOPE

SANDRA A.

DEDICATION

To my husband, John, and to my two wonderful children,
all of whom I have caused so much harm,
I would like to dedicate this book as a "living" amend
to help heal the wounds.
From their unconditional love,
I trust that in time,
I will be forgiven.

CONTENTS

i

ACKNOWLEDGMENTS

For her support, encouragement, and patience with me,
I would like to acknowledge my sister.

She has always believed in me and has taught me to
believe in myself and in a Higher Power.

I would like to thank her for the tedious task of editing
this little book with me.

"You have made known to me

the Path of Life"

Psalms: 16-11

1.   MY EARLY YEARS OF DRINKING

At sixty-eight years of age, I decided it was time to stop killing myself due to my fear of dying and to begin to live. Of course, fear of dying was not my only fear; nor was fear my only reason for drinking. But then, for an alcoholic, anything from extremes of happiness and sorrow and anything in between can serve, in the mind of the alcoholic, as legitimate reasons for drinking.

At the age of 19, I married my high school sweetheart whom I shall refer to as John. Not long after we were married, while living in a one bedroom, one bath apartment in Irving, TX, we made a trip to the neighborhood convenience store and bought a six pack of beer using his fake ID. Had I known anything about alcoholism I would have known then what my future had in store for me because with that first beer I had the most awesome feeling come over me. No longer was I insecure, homely, of average intelligence, a somewhat inhibited and prudish girl. Rather, I was everything I had ever hoped I could be; all those qualities that the 'popular' girls in high school had.

When we realized to have any means at all, John would need to go to college. We moved to Arlington where my husband went to Arlington State College while I worked at a local bank to put him through school. His parents helped out by paying his tuition and books. We both worked hard and drank only occasionally with neighbors who were also students. Things went quite well. John got a B.S. and I managed to collect twelve hours of basic courses that I knew would transfer to The University of Texas in Austin. We moved to Austin so John could continue his studies, earning a M.S. in mathematics and all the class work toward a Ph.D. Again, I worked at a bank to pay for rent and utilities with his parents covering the costs of tuition and books. We took turns working and going to school. I eventually earned a B.A. in history.

John then decided to change fields and went to the School of Library Science. This was a partying group and was comprised primarily of girls and women. Being one of the few men, and the only good looking one, did not want to appear to be a moralist. Since it was the early 70's, I swallowed my morals and did not make a fuss. But that was not all I swallowed. My drinking accelerated considerably because drinking squelched my conscience and allowed me to fit in against my better judgment. I had always been insecure and tried my best to please people in order to win and keep their love and approval. John was no exception; in fact, it was of utmost importance to me to please him. Reader, please understand that I in no way mean to imply that my husband was responsible for my heavy drinking. No one ever forced me to drink. I handled that quite well all by myself.

Somehow as a child, the idea had been engrained in me that my insecurity, that was to stay with me most of my life, could be salved by pleasing those around me. I always felt isolated and alone. About my childhood, I really don't remember very much. I had very wonderful parents; although my memories of their presence in my life are rather sketchy at best. My father was a farmer having to work very hard to eke out a living to feed his family of five children. I had a brother and sister older than myself, 10 and 8 years my senior. Then two sisters were added after me with 4 and 7 years separating us. My mother was busy with household chores and raising her children. She was also very ill all the time. My older sister, and then in time, I had to take up the slack. So I remember a loving environment; although, it was not one that catered to the needs of children. There was a great deal of time to play by myself or with my younger sisters. My older brother and sister had married and moved away when I was about 7 years old.

In school, I got off to a dismal start with an elderly first grade teacher (there was no kindergarten then). On my birthday, she wrote in cursive, which none of us knew how to read, that "Today is Sandra's birthday" or something to that effect. When asked to read what was on the blackboard, I could not, and everyone, though they could not read it either, laughed at me. Being the shy, insecure child that I was, I withdrew further into my shell. This incident just simply set the stage of eleven more years of the same.

As a teenager I was skinny, tall, and pimpled faced. I dated very little and was not at all popular. Of course, those were two strikes against me. I simply withdrew into myself for protection.

While riding on the school bus, I met John. Later I found out that he liked me because I had a ponytail and a letter jacket for basketball. He was much in the same boat as I. He was what would now be called a "nerd" (I think that phrase is still in use). His interests were in science and his IQ tests revealed he was a genius. On the other hand, I was of average intelligence so I thought I had quite a catch. He was tall, dark and handsome; however, he too was not of the popular crowd and thought my athleticism would lend him some credence with the other guys. We dated for two years before he graduated and went to Austin as a freshman at UT. He proceeded to flunk out of his freshman year due to too many extracurricular activities. Out of fear of facing his parents, he ran off to Mexico with the idea of going to Central America and becoming a missionary. Crazy guy! But after two months of bumming around in Mexico, he returned to Texas and to his high school sweetheart. We picked up where we left off.

After earning his MLS in Library Science, John went to work as a Science Bibliographer at the new University of Texas at San Antonio. We bought our first house with the help of his parents who gave us the down payment. It was in a nice neighborhood and we were quite happy now that we had "arrived". I taught Latin in a Catholic High School downtown. After only one year of teaching, I resigned because I had greater things on the way: our first child. We had been married thirteen years and had finally decided we wanted to make a nest and settle down. Our son was born and I became a Mother! Our son bestowed the most important title upon me that I could possibly imagine. I was ecstatic. And then, two years, seven and one half months later, our beautiful daughter was born. I was to never know such happiness as those first years with my children.

John decided, much to my disagreement, that he wanted to leave academia and work for a corporation, a large one in Ft. Worth that had branches nationwide. Sadly, we left San Antonio and returned to the Dallas-Ft. Worth metropolis.   At first, we rented a house until we decided where we wanted to buy. Finally, we bought a lovely two story home in Arlington where we lived the next twenty-five years. Our children attended school from kindergarten through high school in the same system. Our son attended UTA (Arlington) and graduated with a B.S. Our daughter went to UT in Austin also graduating with a B.S.

While renting in Arlington, I was very restless and bored. Neither child was of school age, I knew none of the neighbors. Since I was "only" a renter. I felt an outsider, and therefore, I made no friends. So to fill that hole, I drank; not much, just enough in the afternoon to feel less lonely and bored until John came home from work. Although I played with the children such as reading to them, having art classes, and playing with them outside on their swing set, I still missed adult company. I was a good mother, at least I thought so. I told myself that I never drank too much during this time; though looking back (and I probably knew it then), that is not true. Any amount in the afternoon, alone with two children, was too much. After John got home, he liked to have beer and discuss his day with me while the children played in their rooms. I, too, would have something to drink with him while I listened and made dinner.

When we bought our home and the children were in school, I was quite busy and content volunteering as room mother, a member of the PTA, field trip volunteer, and den mother for the Cub Scouts, etc. I became totally immersed in the lives of my children. Alcohol had no attraction for me at this time.

Then there were cocktail parties that I had to attend connected with John's work. I would get almost sick to my stomach in dread of these. But it was expected of me and so of course I would do it even though I despised playing the social spouse when inside I just wanted to disappear. And therefore, I did what I knew would ease the unease: drink. And what better place to do it than at a cocktail party! I drank somewhat sensibly at these for I did not want to be an embarrassment to John or myself. But, once again, a pattern was set; drink to relieve pressure to be something I was not. After a couple of drinks, I could feel myself metamorphose into that person I so wanted to be; someone who was comfortable in her own skin.

After the children went to junior high school, I found myself more alone again, as children of that age do not want their mothers around so much at school events, or so I thought anyway. Again, I would drink in the afternoon to relieve the loneliness and boredom. I remember a couple of times failing to pick up my daughter and her friend from school because I was taking a nap, alcohol induced, on the sofa and did not awaken in time having set no alarm clock. They had to walk home which was about a mile. My excuse was that I laid down to take a nap and failed to wake up on time. This was true; however, in my heart I knew it was not the whole truth. Such deception alcoholics weave to keep from facing things too painful. I mean I was a "good" mother; good mothers don't take naps and fail to pick up their children. I would have felt guilt even if no alcohol had been involved. But since there was, I felt miserable; though not enough from it happening not once but twice.

About this time, I remember thinking for the first time that I had a drinking problem. I vowed to myself to ease up on the drinking, making rules that I would never drink before five o'clock, I would never drink too much, and on and on. I also remember that I seldom kept these promises to myself for any length of time. Then, I would be vowing the same thing yet again.

.

2. HOW I BECAME AN ALCOHOLIC

I was always a very high functioning alcoholic. At least in my mind, even now, I was. To my knowledge, none of my family suspected I had a problem with alcohol. In addition to this problem, I was very high strung and very sensitive. These traits, I know, affected my family. So it may have been that these traits masked my bad habit of drinking. Of course, at this time in my life, I would not now classify myself as alcoholic. That would come many years later.

At the age of 43, my husband suffered a very devastating stroke; an infarction to the brain stem. He was in a coma for twelve weeks, after which I was able to get him into a rehabilitation hospital. My children were 11 and 8. The family attempted to function as normal. Looking back, I was too proud to ask for help to deal with this blow, although help was offered for my children and for me. "I can handle this" was my mantra. And handle it I did; with the aid of alcohol. Again, I would not categorize myself as alcoholic; but I drank way too much and at inappropriate times.

We somehow survived this period of our lives, at least from my perspective we did. I tried very hard to keep things as normal as possible including things like camping, school events, visiting family and of course, holiday and special day celebrations.

After my husband had been home about three years from the hospital, my father moved in with us. We remodeled the garage into living quarters for him. This put additional stress on me. My father and I were never extremely close; but now I felt I was his little daughter again; someone I had to please and obey. Needless to say, this created considerable resentment in me. How did I handle this? You got it: my best friend, Alcohol. I remember resenting him a great deal when he and his dog would go into the backyard and sit in the swing. Why you might ask? Well, the reason was our entire den was a wall of glass overlooking the backyard. I felt in my paranoid state of mind that he was spying on me and how much I drank and when. Sandra, you are getting very close to being an alcoholic. I can see this as I write this part of my story.

My work load was tremendous. I was a mother of two. I was in charge of all our affairs; not just the usual wife/mother ones. John was completely and totally disabled. I had to do everything for him and I mean everything. My father's presence sometimes was very helpful; for example, I could leave John in bed while I took the kids to school. But later on (he lived with us three and one half years before he died.), due to my drinking, I resented that presence. (One of the amends I was later to make while in A.A. was to my father posthumously. (As I write these lines, Daddy, I realize how much I miss you and would love to relive those years with you.)

In the spring after my father died, John's mother moved in with us because John's father could not take care of her. She was dying with cancer and was in the Hospice program. She died after three months, returning home two days before she died. John's father killed himself five months later. I discovered his body that afternoon when I went to pick him up for his session with the psychologist. I feel he knew I would be the one to find him and clean up the emotional mess he left behind. I was extremely angry. Of course, I drank to numb these emotions.

Reader, can you see the pattern? I, in my insecurity, drank to feel less so. I could not at any time in my life, accept life on its terms. Life should be perfect, whereby I would be happy. If I simply did all the things that I **should** do, then life would be just great. It was my fault that things did not go perfectly. I was imperfect; so I drank to relieve the responsibility I felt. I played God and I was not very good at it. So I drank!

My drinking escalated in the ensuing years, especially after my children were grown and lived away with their spouses. I'm not so sure it was an empty nest syndrome, but rather the old loneliness and boredom. John was always in his study on his computer until I transferred him to bed at night, where he would watch TV shows which did not interest me. I would sit in the living room, watching movies that would depress anyone, and drink. I drank until I was ready for bed. I slept well and awoke ready for a new day; but always disappointed that it was just like the one before. I was in a rut.

3. HOW I BECAME SOBER
(MY FIRST STINT IN A.A.)

This pattern continued. Until, one fateful day after driving my daughter to a law firm in Dallas where she had an interview, I realized I was about out of alcohol. I knew I should not drive anymore for what I had drank that morning really hit me about now. So I went home. I further realized that I had to have a drink and with this realization I knew I would be in no shape to pick up my daughter from her interview. And so I called my son and admitted the horrible truth: "Son, can you go pick up your sister in Dallas because I am drunk and cannot safely drive?" This was one of two phone calls that were the most difficult of things I was ever to do. (The other was a phone call to my daughter many years later of which I shall confess to the reader later). Both calls signaled my entry into A.A. and the beginning of a new life.

When I first entered A.A., I called my son to tell him I was going because I was afraid that I would back out. I had quit drinking on June 6, 2004, but I did not go to A.A. until June 9. Why did I go? I went because in those three days of withdrawal, I was in hell. I was more terrified than I could imagine if I were actually facing the gates of hell. In reality, I suppose in a sense I was.

What ensued over the next year in A.A., was an awakening to life as it could be. I attended a meeting at 6:30 p.m. every night, or so I remember, for the first nine months. I bought and read every book, the Arlington Group had, which were pretty much all of the literature offered by the General Office. I would go home after a meeting, sit in my rocker in our bedroom, and read while John watched TV. The loneliness and boredom disappeared. I was ecstatic with my new life.

Upon returning home after my first meeting where I had admitted those words of freedom: "My name is Sandra and I'm an alcoholic", I ran to John and announced: "I have finally found what I have been searching for all my life." I simply did not realize the profundity of that statement. I had always considered the human condition thusly: "Is this all there is?" Consequently, I was always searching for answers and finding none that had lasting meaning for me, I was more morose than before, and I would drink forgetting the question and therefore no longer needing an answer.

But within the walls of that meeting room of A.A., I heard people sharing their experience, strength, and hope with humility and honesty. I thought "where has all this wisdom been all my life". I felt like such an immature person and realized in time that alcohol had retarded my emotional growth. The wisdom had always been there and most people were living it. Alcohol had simply been my insulation from life and this emotional growth.

Never, except when my children were born, had I experienced anything like this: an absolute love of and an engagement with **life.** I was on a "pink cloud" for my first year at least. I had seldom been so happy.

After three months of sobriety in A.A., our children made it possible for us to go on a cruise. I was very worried that I might start drinking again. I voiced this to my sponsor as well as to the group, and was assured that all I needed to do was to stay spiritually fit and seek out the "Friends of Bill W." aboard ship. This I did and I had a lovely time without worry of wanting a drink.

That first stint in A.A. was lacking one major thing: Step Two, "Came to believe that a Power greater than ourselves could restore us to sanity." Where I sat in that meeting room, I was faced with all the Twelve Steps carved into wooden plaques upon the wall. Quickly upon becoming a member, I noticed that the awful three letter word, GOD, appeared in six of the twelve steps. Being a "devout" atheist, not an agnostic, I recoiled from that part of the program. I spent a great deal of my time in meetings and afterward, arguing with my fellow alcoholic friends. They assured me that my Higher Power could be anything I chose including the A.A. group itself. I felt this a) dishonest and b) lacking intellectual integrity. I saw it as begging the question.

And so I wrestled. Finally, my sponsor suggested that I list the qualities that a god of my understanding might possess. I thought this a childish way of creating god in my own image; but I was desperate to go to any lengths to gain what they in A.A. had to offer: joy, peace, and happiness. And so it was that John and I made a trek to a cabin in the woods near Texarkana. Here I worked non-stop on the literature that I had brought as well as a journal of sorts wherein I would put my thoughts including questions and possible solutions. As my sponsor suggested, I listed the qualities that any entity deserving the title God should possess. These included: unconditional love, compassion, the ability to forgive, kindness and gentleness, an understanding disposition, a sense of fairness, a sense of humor and perhaps others that I can no longer remember. I worked very hard at this task and took it very seriously. When I had finished, I felt I had worked Steps Two and Three. The God of my understanding I named Bona Via, Latin for the good or right path. How very interesting that basically I found the _God of my_ understanding of today. The difference is the hard work! However, the "god" of then was one produced by my head and the God of today is that Deep Reality within all of us.

When I went back to my group meeting, my sponsor was surprised that I had worked Step Three without her assistance. Of course, I was going to do the Steps my way. In fact, in the beginning I told her that I had done Step One when I came into the doors of the Arlington Group of A. A. Furthermore, I felt I needed to skip to Step Four. In order to quit drinking, I must understand why I drank. This Step seemed the most likely Step to accomplish that. Her response was, "No Sandra, we will work the Steps in order!" (It was the end of discussion, happily for me).

So I was very serious about the Steps and the program in so far as I could be at this time in my growth. I remained sober for five years; though much of that time was a "dry sobriety". I had not learned why I drank and I continued in my self-centeredness with all the character defects intact. Why? I did not really have God in my life. I continued playing God.

4. MY "SLIP"

After four years, John and I moved further east and my sister moved west after the death of her husband. We left on bad terms; which was largely if not totally my responsibility. But John and I truly enjoyed our new home and felt somewhat like newlyweds.

In time, one of us decided how nice it would be to have cocktails on the back porch in the afternoon, with the ceiling fan going, watching the ripples made by a southerly breeze undulating on the small lake catching the sunlight and providing us with a light show. It was a near perfect picture; all that was missing were two cocktail glasses on the bistro table between us.

When first we went to the liquor store about six miles from our house, I parked in the parking lot and felt a bit of trepidation and told John that I did not think it a good idea to go inside. However, I did not stay with that initial warning. The next day found us parked in the same spot with my going into the establishment and purchasing him a bottle of Southern Comfort and myself a bottle of Scotch, my drink of choice. I practically raced home to pour that elixir into those waiting glasses. Oh how sweet! We had two drinks as I had promised myself we would do. But I had allowed myself to believe that I could handle it. I wanted to believe. I forgot all that I had learned five years ago at A. A. Arlington Group. Step One: "We admitted to ourselves that we were **powerless** over alcohol and that our lives had become unmanageable."

What was I thinking? Why did I permit myself this slip? Well, it did not continue with two drinks. It built up to three, then four. Finally, I thought I was not doing too well drinking moderately; so, I decided to switch to wine. No harm in that, I told myself. The sad thing about being an alcoholic is that one is an expert at self-deception. I could believe anything that I told myself when it came to the subject of alcohol.

How did the wine experiment go you might ask? About like Bill W.'s beer experiment, it flopped! Soon I was drinking almost as badly as when I went to A. A. in 2004. I began drinking during this slip in May, 2009. I told my son in September 2009 that we were drinking cocktails out on the back porch. He said with tears in his eyes: "Oh, Mom, don't you know you are an alcoholic and that you cannot drink. Don't you remember how proud all of us were of you each time you collected one of those chips? Now, I have to worry about your showing up at my wedding drunk. [He was to be married in April, 2010.] Crying, I promised him that I would quit and that he need not worry. He was visibly relieved.

I kept my promise for a time. Then I began to drink again and this time being very secretive about it once more. I went to different liquor stores (there were three close together) so that no one would be the wiser as to how much I was drinking. A friend of mine owned one of the stores.

When the children came to see me, I would be sure that no empties were in the trash and I would make sure I had a good hiding place for my five liter box of wine; but in a place that I could get a nip should I be in need of one.

Once, my daughter came to visit with my two grandchildren. Before she arrived, I took a few ounces of John's Southern Comfort to quiet my nerves. Well, my daughter is more perceptive than John or my son; i.e. with her it is harder to hide my drinking. She was extremely upset with me, as well she should have been.

In July 2010, the children decided that they would have nothing to do with me, including letting me see the grandchildren, until I stopped drinking. I was livid. How dare they control my life, I told myself! So to spite them, I just drank that much more. Oh what stupid thinking!

Things just continued to get worse and worse. I would, after a particularly bad binge, cease. The withdrawals got worse and worse as well. I had convinced my children that I was not drinking that much and that I would like for them to continue to visit. Then one day, my daughter and my grandchildren are on their way from Dallas to visit. I call her about 9:00 a.m. to see if she has left. She had and was in Rockwall. I thought that I had time for another glass of wine before she got there and would be okay when she arrived. But lo and behold, it hit me like a rock! I called her again and told her I was drunk and not to bring the children. She was only thirty minutes away from my home.

How could I do that, you might ask? Why could I not, for the sake of seeing my beloved daughter and grandchildren, just not have had that first glass of wine that morning at all? There is an explanation in <u>Alcoholics Anonymous,</u> Fourth Edition, pg. 24: ***"The fact is that most alcoholics, for reasons yet obscure, have lost the power of choice in drink. Our so-called will power becomes practically nonexistent. We are unable, at certain times, to bring into our consciousness with sufficient force the memory of the suffering and humiliation of even a week or a month ago. We are without defense against the first drink.***"

Even now, several weeks later, one month sober, I cannot express the regret for the harm I caused her that day. How cruel! How mean! How dreadful. I could go on and on and still not come close to describing the horror of that day for her.

5. HOW I BECAME SOBER AND WORKED STEPS TWO AND THREE

That incident was on a Sunday. On Monday, I had a glass of wine upon awakening and vowed I would quit. Once again, I went through three days of utter hell as the withdrawals set in. Probably, I should have gone to a hospital to detox. But, what would I do about John, who was in bed? All sorts of possible solutions went through my head, but none seemed to work. So, I lay in bed for twenty-four hours getting up only to vomit into a basin I kept beside the bed. Of course, there were chills, then sweat. There was some shaking as well. But the scariest thing was the heart palpitations. I thought "I am going to die".

That was on Monday, July 11, 2011. It is of this writing August 11, 2011 one month of sobriety. One month of freedom from the tyrant, alcohol. But the most miraculous thing that has happened to me in that month has been I, for the first time, have truly, with my heart so to speak, worked Steps Two and Three, as well as all the others with that three letter word in it. Finally, I am happy, joyous, and free. I had to "let go absolutely." "Half measures availed us nothing". [Alcoholics Anonymous, Fourth Edition, pgs. 58-59.]

I was willing to go to any lengths to get what they, the members of A.A., had. I got online as soon as I could walk to my computer and type. I searched for nearby meetings. Thankfully, I found an excellent one in Mt. Vernon and they permitted me to bring John into the meeting. I could not leave him alone due to his disability.

To be an alcoholic is something no one wants to be. As is mentioned in our text, "Alcoholics Anonymous", affectionately called the "Big Book", if we had a disease such as cancer, our family and friends would be more understanding, more supportive. One sister could not believe that I did not have the sense or the will power to just not drink if it meant whether or not I would see my daughter and grandchildren. In the "Big Book", in the Chapter to Employers, page 138, it describes how a person who can drink moderately cannot understand the alcoholic. "*As a moderate drinker, you can take your liquor or leave it alone. Whenever you want to, you control your drinking. Of an evening, you can go on a mild bender, get up in the morning, shake your head and go to business. To you, liquor is no real problem. You cannot see why it should be to anyone else, save the* **spineless and stupid"** [emphasis mine].

Let there be no mistake! The excerpt above in no way relieves me of my responsibility for harm done to those important in my life. Bill W. puts it very aptly when he states: "The alcoholic is like a tornado roaring his way through the lives of others." [Alcoholics Anonymous, Fourth Edition, pg. 82]

I am willing to make amends to all those I have harmed. But simply because I am ready, it does not follow that those I have emotionally devastated with my drinking are ready to accept those amends. I pray for the day when they might be able to accept and forgive. Meantime, I am doing a "living" amend by not drinking.

6. WHAT LIFE IS LIKE NOW

Perhaps, the most important thing I have learned is that pain and suffering caused by drinking brings about surrender. Surrender brings about humility. In a humble frame of mind, I am able to keep close to the Mind of God.

Since I have been sober, there have been many emotional upsets. However, instead of playing God, I am willing to have Him run the show. During the first few days without alcohol, I sang over and over a hymn from my childhood:

"Have thine own way Lord,

have thine own way.

Thou art the potter, I am the clay.

Mold me and make me,

after thy will,

while I am waiting, yielded, and still."

I am truly happy. Something else I have learned is that life does not have to be such that I am always happy. Life is a messy sort of thing sometimes. I don't have to fix it. I must accept things the way they are, people the way they are, and myself the way I am. This of course brings to mind Reinhold Niebuhr's famous prayer:

God, grant me the Serenity <u>to accept</u> the

things I cannot change,

the Courage <u>to change</u> the things I can,

and the Wisdom <u>to know</u> the difference.

I have written this book for two reasons: **#1** It is my way of working Step Twelve: "Having had a spiritual awakening as the result of these steps, we tried to carry this message to alcoholics and to practice these principles in all our affairs". **#2** It is my way of working Step Nine: "Made direct amends to such people wherever possible, except when to do so would injure them or others". To work Step Nine would be to attempt yet once again to force my will on those not yet ready to accept amends. It would be putting my self's misery at ease; but, it would be injurious to those to whom I have caused enough emotional distress. I choose to live with that fact and let go, and as they say in A. A., let God.

When we have done our direct amends as suggested in Step Nine, *"if we are painstaking about this phase of our development, we will be amazed before we are half way through. We are going to know a new freedom and a new happiness. We will not regret the past nor wish to shut the door on it. We will comprehend the word serenity and we will know peace. No matter how far down the scale we have gone, we will see how our experience can benefit others. That feeling of usefulness and self-pity will disappear. We will lose interest in selfish things and gain interest in our fellows. Self-seeking will slip away. Our whole attitude and outlook upon life will change. Fear of people and of economic insecurity will leave us. We will intuitively know how to handle situations which used to baffle us. We will suddenly realize that God is doing for us what we could not do for ourselves."* [Alcoholics Anonymous, Fourth Edition, pgs. 83-84] This passage is known in A.A. as "The Promises".

I have come to realize that all my life I have been seeking something greater than myself. Carl Jung, a psychotherapist who had a great influence on A.A. formation, coined the phrase "spiritus contra spiritum". Having taught Latin, this phrase intrigued me. With the help of the internet, since my memory failed me in this endeavor, I searched for a proper translation in the context in which he used this phrase. A rough translation might be something like "Spirit ravaged by spirits", [of the bottle]. Wow, this had a profound effect upon me. I realized that the searching I had spent a greater part of my adult life was a seeking after my true nature and to find that "Spirit" with which to make the two whole. When frustrated in my efforts, primarily because I sought too hard rather than being open and willing to receive, I drank 'spirits' to fill that hole.

Furthermore, I see that my true nature is to help people. I am a caring person who truly wants to reach out to people in need. However, my past history has been to do so for the wrong reasons. My motivation was to win love and approval from those I helped. In keeping with my true nature and yet to remain whole, I find I want to help others now because I want to express outwardly that inward nature, the nature of the God of my understanding. In so doing, I become one with that Deep Reality. For in order for God to be essential, it needs me. Likewise, for me to be essential, I need God. Thusly, the outward me reflects the inward me. I am no longer such a split person; I am finding that wholeness for which I have been seeking. Similar to working the Steps, this new state of consciousness of awareness of my true self versus the false self of ego, is a work in progress; for I strive toward progress not perfection.

7. THERE IS A SOLUTION

If in reading this, you identify with me as an alcoholic I would like to suggest to you that there is a solution. Go to an A. A. meeting. Sit and observe only, if you do not wish to share. You will know if you are an alcoholic when you hear the others sharing their stories. If you decide that indeed you are an alcoholic, and "if you have decided that you want what we have and are willing to go to any length to get it, then you are ready to take certain steps." [<u>Alcoholics</u> <u>Anonymous,</u> Fourth Edition, pg. 58]

It is a wonderful solution. It is like taking a veil from your eyes. I came out of a fog, the veil was removed, and I saw, for the first time, what life could be. I awake in the morning joyously anticipating what the day holds for me. If it turns out not to be so good, then I can tell myself, that's okay. And I can look to the God of my understanding for help. The help comes in the form of getting out of self and opening up to that Deep Reality within us all. It is an inclusive program. No particular brand of religion, in fact, no religion at all is suggested. It is indeed a spiritual program but not a religious one.

Due to the God of my understanding, the A. A. group, the meetings, the Twelve Steps, and meditation, I am becoming emotionally sober. That is quite an accomplishment. I strive toward progress, not perfection. I need be perfect only with respect to Step One: ...***powerless over alcohol***.

I pray that I may keep close to the mind of God.

God, grant me the grace to accept with serenity

the things I cannot change,

the courage to change the things I can,

and the wisdom to know the difference.

....Reinhold Niebuhr

ABOUT THE AUTHOR

My name is Sandra and I am an Alcoholic. I have always wanted to write and publish a book. However, I had no intention of writing a book on alcoholism. Somewhere I read that one should write about what one knows best. Unfortunately, I have first-hand experience on the subject. If this book can help one who is or is soon to be an alcoholic, then it will be a good thing. I am grateful for the A. A. Fellowship.

I live in East Texas with my husband, John. We have two children who live in the Dallas metropolis. Our daughter gave us two grandchildren whom we adore. And from our son we may soon expect additional little ones. For my family, I am deeply grateful.

www.ingramcontent.com/pod-product-compliance
Lightning Source LLC
Chambersburg PA
CBHW031329290526
45784CB00014B/2454